april pulley sayre

BLOOM BOOM!

BEACH LANE BOOKS
New York London Toronto Sydney New Delhi

Every spring,
across the land. . . .

Seeds sprout.

Stems pop out.

Bloom,
boom!

Leaves
emerge.

Stalks surge.

Bloom,
boom!

Plants rise.

Shapes surprise.

Bloom,
boom!

Bulbs
send.

Tips extend.

Bloom,
boom!

Buds grow.

Blossoms show.

Bloom,
boom!

Petals curve.

Insects swerve.

Bloom,
boom!

Colors
call.

Fragrance flies.

Welcome, birds
and butterflies!

Sun rays warm.

Flowers form.

Bloom . . .

BOOM!

The Bloom Boom

In spring, flowering plants can bloom a few at a time, over weeks and months.
But sometimes, many bloom all at once. There's a *boom* of blooms.

Desert Bloom

In deserts of the southwestern United States, spring desert bloom depends on rainfall and air temperatures during the previous winter. Rain moistens seeds that lie in the soil—even soil that looks like sandy, bare ground. These seeds sprout, put down roots, and form stems, leaves, and flowers.

After the flowers bloom, they quickly form seeds. The new seeds drop to the soil, ready for the next rains. These plants are called annuals because they pack their entire lifetime, from seed to flower to seed, into less than one year. When the plant dies, its seeds remain. Some annuals called desert ephemerals fit this entire cycle into only a few weeks or even days!

Being an annual does not mean these plants bloom *every* year. The next major rains may arrive in a year, or after decades. Deserts also have perennials. Perennials, including shrubs, agave, and cacti, survive year-to-year as full plants or roots and stems, not just seeds.

Lupine and Bluebonnet Meadows

Hundreds of species of lupine, known for their tall flower spikes, grow in North America, South America, and Europe. Texas bluebonnets are species of lupine that bring a sea of blue to the hills and roadways of Texas. Bluebonnets and other lupines are wildflowers, but they are helped along by gardeners, highway maintenance crews, and park staff, who spread the seeds.

From Maine to California and far beyond, lupines are a favorite wildflower and garden plant—and not just because of the flowers. The symmetrical, hairy leaves hold raindrops, making them look bejeweled after storms.

Wildflowers of the Woodlands

From trillium to lady's slippers, woodland wildflowers display surprising shapes and colors. White, pink, red, blue, and yellow spring flowers decorate forests in the eastern and midwestern United States. As with other bloom booms, this one is all about timing. The wildflowers gather energy from sunlight that reaches their leaves before the trees overhead leaf out and bloom. During this time, pollinators such as bees, beetles, bee flies, and other flies visit them on the forest floor, before these insects shift their attention to the tree blossoms high above. Woodland wildflowers tend to be perennials. Some, such as the jack-in-the-pulpit, may grow for as many as seven years before they have the energy to form a flower.

Tulip and Daffodil Displays

City landscapers and home gardeners create bloom booms with tulips, daffodils, and other bulbs. Bulbs are not seeds. They are underground storage structures that consist mostly of a plant's bud and leaf and a bit of stem. Most tulip bulbs are grown on large farms in Michigan, Iowa, Washington State, and in the country of Holland. Wild tulip bulbs are native to Turkey, parts of North Africa, the Middle East, and Asia. For hundreds of years, tulips have been bred and crossbred to create many different shapes and colors. During the Dutch tulip craze in the early 1600s, the flowers were so popular that people made and lost huge fortunes buying and selling tulip bulbs.

Redbud and Dogwood Bloom

In the eastern half of the United States, forests blaze with pink and white flowers in spring. This is the redbud and dogwood bloom. (Despite their name, redbud tree blooms are lavender to pink.) Redbuds and dogwoods are understory trees. That means they are shorter than the mature oaks, hickories, and beech trees that may grow above them.

Redbuds and dogwoods bloom just after the woodland wildflowers. They, too, can take advantage of the pollinators that are not yet buzzing around the flowers of taller trees. Redbuds produce some flowers right on their branches and even on their trunks, not on long stems and shoots like most plants. This way of producing flowers is called cauliflory.

Flowering Landscape Trees

Redbuds and dogwoods aren't the only prized spring trees. All around the world, landscapers plant cherry trees, crabapples, magnolias, Bradford pears, and other fragrant, flowering ornamental trees. People love to stroll beneath the colorful blooms and the flower petals that fall from the trees when the wind blows.

Poppy Bloom

California poppies and desert gold poppies bloom in the deserts of Utah, California, and Arizona, and in the hills near Los Angeles and San Diego. California poppies may be annual or perennial, depending on local conditions.

The Flowers and the Feast

The wildflower boom is a time of feasting. Bees, flies, beetles, butterflies, hummingbirds, and bats feed on nectar or pollen produced by flowers. Indeed, the plants produce flowers—with all these colors, shapes, smells, and sweet treats—in order to lure pollinators, creatures that will carry their pollen from plant to plant.

Swapping pollen with another plant helps create strong, varied seeds. So flowers have structures that dab or sprinkle pollen on the creatures that visit them. Close to the ground, some flowers give off stinky, rotten smells to attract their pollinators: beetles and flies.

This buzz of activity attracts insect eaters. In deserts and drylands, lizards abound, gobbling insects attracted by the blooms. Chickadees and warblers flit among the branches of woodland flowering trees, probing each bud and flower for caterpillars and other small insects. Hummingbirds hover at flowers, nabbing gnats and small flies.

Bloom Booms Around the World

Spring isn't the only bloom time. The peak of flower bloom in the tallgrass prairie is July and August. Wildflower meadows high up in the mountains of Colorado and Washington State may not reach full bloom until July or later. Rain forest trees bloom many months of the year. And deserts have flowers that bloom in summer, as well.

Global climate change is affecting some weather patterns, making bloom times shift in response to droughts or unusually heavy rains. So when seeking bloom booms, it's helpful to know about recent weather and rainfall. To learn more about flower blooms, a good place to start is your local nature center, native plant society, or botanical garden.

Bloom Resources

American Horticultural Society (ahsgardening.org) has youth gardening programs, a directory of gardens, and gardening resources.

American Public Gardens Association (publicgardens.org) has a searchable list of public gardens.

Botanic Gardens Conservation International (bgci.org) works with botanical gardens worldwide to help conserve plants.

Desert USA (desertusa.com) has updated wildflower reports for western parks and roadsides.

Native Plant Societies

Native plant society members tend to know local plants and when they bloom. Search the Internet for "native plant society" and your state's name, or look at the list on the American Horticulture Society's website: ahsgardening.org/gardening-resources/societies-clubs-organizations/native-plant-societies.

A Bit More About the Blooms

California poppy (*Eschscholzia californica*) is the state flower of California. Even though their common name is "poppy," the California poppy and desert gold poppy are not "true" poppies. (True poppies are members of the genus *Papaver* and one species is the source of poppy seeds in baked goods.)

Wild lupine (*Lupinus perennis*) grows in the Midwest. The invertebrate pictured is a millipede.

Desert globe mallow (*Sphaeralcea ambigua*) is often called the desert hollyhock because its tall stems resemble hollyhocks, a garden plant also in the mallow family.

An eastern cottontail rabbit sits among wild lupine. Young cottontail rabbits have a blaze of white fur on their forehead. Older cottontails do not.

The blue, bell-shaped desert Canterbury bell or desert bell (*Phacelia campanularia*) grows in sandy, gravelly places, such as the edges of desert washes, where water flows after rains.

Bloodroot (*Saguinaria canadensis*) flowers push through oak leaves in a forest in spring. The roots of these woodland wildflowers contain a reddish sap, hence the name.

Pink lady's slipper (*Cypripedium acaule*) is a native orchid that grows in shade under trees, often pine trees. It should never be picked. Many native orchids are protected by law because they are uncommon, take years to grow, and do not transplant well.

California poppy, shown sprouting here, is often planted by seed in western gardens.

Desert gold poppy (*Eschscholzia glyptosperma*) is yellow and grows amid other wildflowers in the Sonoran Desert near Phoenix.

The prefix "tri" in white trillium (*Trillium grandiflorum*) is a hint to identifying this plant. These woodland flowers have three petals.

Stalks of purple Arizona lupine (*Lupinus arizonicus*) grow among desert gold poppies and clusters of golden chia, also called California sage (*Salvia columbariae*). Golden chia seeds are used to make pinole, a traditional food of southwestern native people. The chia seeds found in grocery stores are from a closely related plant.

Tulips (genus *Tulipa*) grow from bulbs. They are perennials and may come back year after year.

There are at least 3,000 varieties of tulips because gardeners have been crossbreeding these flowers for centuries.

Raindrops cover the bud of a magnolia (genus *Magnolia*) tree.

Eastern redbud (*Cercis canadensis*) bears pink to lavender flowers, not red ones, despite its name.

Eastern redbud is a wild, medium-sized tree in American forests, but is also planted in gardens. It forms long brown pods and is in the pea family.

Magnolias that are pink or purple are sometimes called Japanese magnolias, but they are originally from China.

Wild lupine provides nectar for bumblebees. Caterpillars of the endangered Karner blue butterfly eat only this kind of lupine.

Texas loves its bluebonnets (*Lupinus texensis*). Several species of lupine that grow in Texas are called bluebonnets, and all are official state flowers.

Pink dogwood is a variety of flowering dogwood (*Cornus florida*), a plant native to the United States and Mexico. The symmetrical, four-petaled flowers produce red fruits that feed cardinals, waxwings, and other birds.

Crabapple trees (genus *Malus*) are offspring of the original wild apples that were bred to create the large apples sold in grocery stores. These ornamental trees bear white or pink fragrant flowers and produce colorful tiny apples that wild birds eat in late winter.

A black-capped chickadee feeds among the flowers of a crabapple tree.

A cabbage white butterfly rests on a magnolia flower. Magnolias range from small shrub size to tree-sized.

A common side-blotched lizard warms up on a rock before going out to feed on insects lured by desert wildflowers.

The bluish purple blooms of desert hyacinth, also called blue dicks (*Dichelostemma capitatum*), grow among California poppies.

California poppies coat hillsides near Los Angeles with orange in early spring.

For Tish and Pearl, from your flower girl

THANK YOU to the St. Joseph County Parks and all
other national, state, county, and city parks
that preserve wildflower habitat. Thank you,
Wendy C. Hodgson, herbarium curator
and senior research botanist of the Desert
Botanical Garden in Phoenix, Arizona, for
reviewing the text. Thank you to research
scientist Philip C. Rosen of University of
Arizona, Mike Plagens, and Megan Jessop.
Thank you to Andrea Welch, Lauren "Raindrops"
Rille, Allyn Johnston, Sarah Jane Abbott, Elizabeth
Blake-Linn, Bridget Madsen, and the rest of the Beach Lane/S&S
team. Thank you to Rodney Willett for photographing the lady's
slippers for this book—and for being such a great brother-in-law.
Love and gratitude to native plant expert Jeff Sayre for text review,
wildflower adventures, and the desert bell photo on this page.

BEACH LANE BOOKS

An imprint of Simon & Schuster Children's Publishing Division
1230 Avenue of the Americas, New York, New York 10020
Copyright © 2019 by April Pulley Sayre
For information about special discounts for bulk purchases, please contact Simon & Schuster Special Sales at 1-866-506-1949
or business@simonandschuster.com. • The Simon & Schuster Speakers Bureau can bring authors to your live event. For more
information or to book an event, contact the Simon & Schuster Speakers Bureau at 1-866-248-3049 or visit our website at
www.simonspeakers.com. • Book design by Lauren Rille • The text for this book was set in Lunchbox. • Manufactured in China •
0319 SCP • 10 9 8 7 6 5 4 3 2
Library of Congress Cataloging-in-Publication Data
Names: Sayre, April Pulley, author. • Title: Bloom boom! / April Pulley Sayre. • Description: First edition. | New York : Beach
Lane Books, 2019. | Includes bibliographical references and index. • Identifiers: LCCN 2018016840 | ISBN 9781481494724
(hardcover : alk. paper) | ISBN 9781481494731 (eBook) • Subjects: LCSH: Flowers—Juvenile literature. • Classification: LCC
QK49 .S32 2019 | DDC 581—dc23 LC record available at https://lccn.loc.gov/2018016840